ANNE HOOPER

YOUR
Secret
SEX
DIARY

DK

A DK PUBLISHING BOOK

Created and produced by
CARROLL & BROWN LIMITED
5 Lonsdale Road
London UK NW6 6RA

Publishing Director Denis Kennedy
Art Director Chrissie Lloyd

Editor Joel Levy
Designer Paul Stradling

Production Wendy Rogers

US Editor Laaren Brown

First American Edition, 1997
2 4 6 8 10 9 7 5 3 1

Published in the United States by DK Publishing , Inc.
95 Madison Avenue, New York, New York 10016
Visit us on the World Wide Web at http://www.dk.com

Copyright © 1997 Dorling Kindersley Limited, London
Text copyright © 1997 Anne Hooper

ISBN 0-7894-1469-4

*While every effort has been made to trace the copyright holders of the quotations in this publication,
Carroll and Brown apologize for any omissions that may inadvertently have occurred.*

Reproduced by Colourscan, Singapore
Printed in Hong Kong by Wing King Tong

CONTENTS

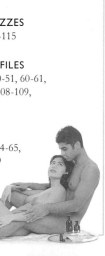

INTRODUCTION 4-5

THE LOVER'S YEAR 6-127

Including:

INTRODUCTION

PERSONAL DIARIES are traditionally the most secret and trusted of confidantes. In them we record not just events but feelings and emotions that we would hesitate to reveal anywhere else. But few of us have extended this degree of personal openness to sexuality. There are some notorious historical and literary examples of people (mainly men) who have laid bare their every encounter, but how many of us have created our own "X-rated" documents?

Of course we are all private human beings. We don't necessarily want the world to know what we are up to in the hidden regions of the mind, not to mention the body. We may be particularly shy of our nearest and dearest knowing our innermost secrets. This book, however, is designed to provide you with the privacy you need to relax and open up.

You may be surprised at the effect that recording your thoughts and fantasies can achieve. It could make you much more confident about realizing these secret desires, or allow you to look back over your year and assess the course your love life has taken. If you choose to keep the diary along with your lover, it could help you explore new sexual territories and discover new heights of passion and eroticism.

With this very special diary, we are giving you – man or woman – the opportunity to create your own very special sexual document – a unique record that you'll want to return to again and again.

To jolt your creativity we offer, on the following pages, hints and tips about aspects of sexuality, and space to record the most personal aspects of your sex life. The weeks have not been tied in to specific months of the year, because I believe you might prefer to have the choice of starting this record at a particularly passionate time in your life.

So, as you put pen to paper, remember that this secret erotic diary is for your eyes only. Throw away your inhibitions and put down . . . anything!

Anne Hooper

WEEK
beginning.................................

Monday

Tuesday

Wednesday

Thursday

Friday

Saturday

"I used to be Snow White, but I drifted."
Mae West

Sunday

My Five Favorite Fantasies

In your fantasies, you can let yourself go completely. But most of us are wary of disclosing these most secret stories, even if we trust our lovers.

This is where the secret diary comes in. Below we suggest some all-time favorite scenarios to get you going.

HER:
Sex slave to primitive king
Sex with a stranger
Seduced by lesbian
Exhibitionist in the street
Dominatrix with sex slave

HIM:
Being seduced by an older woman
Nurse in uniform
Hooker offers all for free
French maid in uniform
Watching lesbians

Note down your favorite fantasies:

1 ....

2 ....

3 ....

4 ....

5 ....

WEEK
beginning...............................

Monday

Tuesday

Wednesday

Thursday

Friday

Saturday

> "Give a man a free hand, and he'll run it all over you."
> *Mae West*

Sunday

❧ *The* DYNAMIC *lover*

The dynamic lover is an exhilarating individual who charges any situation with exciting, spontaneous energy. You will very often come up with something bold, new, and shocking; in the bedroom or in everyday life. Life is never dull with a man or a woman who is gifted with this energetic brand of dynamism. But beware of going too far. You may have a habit of overlooking the needs and personality of your lover when you devote all your energy to absorbing schemes. Maybe you should spend more time asking what would please and captivate your partner, and less on yourself. But your partner should not let this distract him or her from the excitement and exuberance you can bring to almost every aspect of sexuality, love and life.

WEEK
beginning..

Monday

....

Tuesday

....

Wednesday

....

Thursday

....

Friday

LOVE FACTS: *Falling in Love*

LOVE AT FIRST SIGHT

There's no definite explanation for this phenomenon, but people who are similar in physical attractiveness are likely to feel they make a good match, and each may feel ready for a powerful emotional event.

FEAR AND LOVING

Fear and anxiety can often prove to be excellent stimulants for falling in love. Sharing a dangerous experience can create an extremely powerful force of attraction.

ALL AT SEA

It may be a cliché, but one of the best ways to meet someone and fall in love is to take a cruise. You will spend time at close quarters with convivial people under relaxed circumstances, and research has shown that you are most likely to be attracted to someone from your immediate environment. So if you are looking for love, book yourself a passage on board ship now!

Saturday

Sunday

"Love doesn't make the world go round. Love is what makes the ride worthwhile."
Franklin Jones

WEEK
beginning.....................................

Monday

....

Tuesday

....

Wednesday

....

Thursday

....

Friday

Saturday

Sunday

CAPRICORN *lovers*

SHE values a partner's fidelity, although she may stray once or twice herself. Her pragmatic nature, however, enables her to deal with her man's occasional wayward affair, provided she truly believes he loves her. Although Capricorn woman's approach to sex can be businesslike, she is not averse to indulging in wild fantasies from time to time. In bed she prefers not to be on top, and likes side-by-side positions and oral sex. She loves to hear her man moan during sex.

HE has a very earthy approach to sex. He is not a big fan of extended foreplay, preferring the solid security of lovemaking in the missionary position. But he definitely enjoys a good laugh in bed and believes that lovemaking should primarily be about having fun, in a straightforward way.

WEEK
beginning.................................

Monday

....

Tuesday

....

Wednesday

....

Thursday

....

Friday

The SENSITIVE *lover*

Sensitivity can be both an asset and a liability. As a sensitive lover you make a wonderful partner because you are always thinking about what will please or displease your lover. However, extreme sensitivity can create such a high degree of anxiety that you may become metaphorically paralyzed about taking sexual action. You need to be bolder about lovemaking in order to free yourself of petty, stifling fears. This will open you up to some of the delights of uninhibited sex. If you can become more self-assured, you have the potential to be among the most arousingly erotic of partners. Turn your sensitive nature to your advantage by making it into a sensual one.

Saturday

Sunday

"I like to wake up each morning feeling a new man."
Jean Harlow

HOW *erotic* A

Do you prefer to

a talk dirty?
b take your time with foreplay?
c get down to sex immediately?

Does sexual suggestion

a make you hot and excited?
b work if you're in the right mood?
c leave you cold?

If lust strikes you in public, do you

a feel even sexier because you can't make love?
b wait until you get home?
c fall on each other in the nearest doorway?

Do you show sexual interest by

a dropping suggestive hints?
b using your body provocatively?
c saying so?

Are you most highly aroused by

a being forced to wait?
b stopping and starting sex?
c prolonged sexual intercourse?

Is your sensual preference

a being stroked all over the body?
b having your lover stroke your genitals?
c stroking your own genitals?

LOVER ARE YOU?

HOW DID YOU SCORE?

Mostly ⓐ answers
SUBTLE

You like it when eroticism has been built up to such a level that it only takes a sexy look to make you feel weak at the knees. Sexual games really appeal since, for you, good sex happens in the brain.

Go to "The Subtle Lover" on page 25.

Mostly ⓑ answers
ENTHUSIASTIC

You love the idea of playing sex games but tend to get hijacked by your enthusiasm for intercourse. Try to deliberately wait a while before intercourse and build on those erotic feelings.

Turn to "The Enthusiastic Lover" on page 45.

Mostly ⓒ answers
DIRECT

You are uncomplicated enough to be able to get enormous satisfaction from the act of intercourse alone. Sex is, for you, a healthy pastime – provided you discover the right partner.

See "The Direct Lover" on page 61.

WEEK
beginning..............................

Monday

....

Tuesday

....

Wednesday

....

Thursday

....

Friday

The PLEASING *lover*

Everyone loves a pleasing lover like you because you are so agreeable to spend time with. The problem with this is that if you are concentrating only on pleasing other people, many of your own needs may get lost along the way. But there can be real difficulty with changing your pleasing ways. If you deliberately become more selfish and care only about your own affairs, others may react with annoyance. Striking some sort of a balance (between a selfish approach and considering others) is a very important task, but certainly not an easy one. But it is worth the effort. Although it may go against your instincts, you will be better off in the long run. When you are happier, your lover will also be happier.

Saturday

Sunday

"I think the people who like sex stay home. I mean they don't make a big thing out of it."
Nelson Algren

WEEK
beginning.................................

Monday

....

Tuesday

....

Wednesday

....

Thursday

....

Friday

Saturday

Sunday

AQUARIUS *lovers*

♂ HE adores the notion of wild and kinky sex, but at the same time he fears losing control. He may find it very difficult to actually climax. His perfect woman practices amazing, sensual massage complemented by an extremely rich and active fantasy life. Aquarius man has a tendency to concentrate too much on his partner's pleasure, rather than his own.

♀ SHE is extremely responsive and can be wonderfully sensuous and erotic. But she is also preoccupied with her public image and would hesitate to do anything that made her appear overly eager. What really turns Aquarius woman on is money, although she's also into kinky sex, including bondage and mild S & M – as long as it's kept discreet.

WEEK
beginning.....................................

Monday

Tuesday

Wednesday

Thursday

Friday

Saturday

> "A woman should put perfume on the places where she wants to be kissed."
> *Coco Chanel*

Sunday

 Things That Turn Me On/Off

A very common belief about sex is that we all like the same things. But of course we don't. Each of us has a unique pathway into good sex that consists of a combination of moves, thoughts, and suggestions that turns us on. Likewise there are dislikes. What is one man's aphrodisiac can be another man's passion-killer.

SOME CLASSIC TURN-ONS:
Romantic talk
Dirty talk
Verbal fantasies

All-over body stroking
Sensual massage
Genital stimulation
Scratching and biting

What turns you on?

1 ....

2 ....

3 ....

What turns you off?

1 ....

2 ....

3 ....

WEEK
beginning.................................

Monday

....

Tuesday

....

Wednesday

....

Thursday

....

Friday

The SUBTLE lover

The subtle lover is a master of eroticism because a subtle mind can take hold of fine nuances of suggestion and allow them to develop into something creative and different. You are fortunate in having such a distinctive imagination linked with the ability to understand your unique and special sexual impact. The downside is that as a subtle lover you may come to require elaborate fantasies for total satisfaction. A major task in life, therefore, is to discover a partner whose inventiveness and imagination match up – a mind and personality that complement your own. This will not always be easy, but it's definitely worth holding out for the right person. Together you can explore an exciting world of luscious sensuality and pure eroticism that most couples desire but never attain.

Saturday

Sunday

WEEK

beginning...................................

Monday

....

Tuesday

....

Wednesday

....

Thursday

....

Friday

Hot Spots

There are areas of the human body, known as erogenous zones, which, if caressed and stimulated, feel erotic. Imagine your lover's body as a map and do the Map Test with your fingertips. Touch every part of your lover's body and ask her to describe how it feels.

SOME TOP LOVERS' HOT SPOTS:
Inner thighs
Behind the ears
Around the genitals

Nipples
Soles of the feet
Nape of the neck
Buttocks

His top three hot spots:

1 ....

2 ....

3 ....

Her top three hot spots:

1 ....

2 ....

3 ....

Saturday

Sunday

"If you cannot be chaste, be cautious."
Spanish proverb

WEEK
beginning.................................

Monday

....

Tuesday

....

Wednesday

....

Thursday

....

Friday

Saturday

. . . .

Sunday

PISCES *lovers*

♂ HE has a tendency to treat sex like some sort of exam subject, methodically working through every position in the manual. This might make him seem faintly ridiculous, but the upside is that he is a great sex partner and willing to learn. He can be indecisive in other respects, though.

♀ SHE is filled with dreams and desires that she may not have the confidence or strength of resolve to achieve. Pisces woman is a genuinely nice person who would benefit from tuition in the outer reaches of eroticism. If she is lucky enough to receive this, she can overcome her timidity and become a rare prize. Given this sort of attention, Pisces woman can get over her shy disposition and reveal her true desires. On the whole she favours woman-on-top positions and likes to lie face down. She quickly gets bored by the missionary position.

Did you feel the HEAT?

DANGER ZONE!

RED HOT!

HOT

HEATING UP

WARM

GETTING
WARMER

COOL

This is the first of three orgasm charts to help you make a record of your sexual year. Use it to keep track of your orgasmic experiences. Write the date you had the orgasm in one of the colored bands on the Cool – Danger Zone! scale and add the sticker symbol that best defines the orgasm you had.

ORGASMIC SYMBOLS

Individual
Simultaneous
Prolonged
Multiple

LOVER'S NAME

HOW *realistic*

If you fell in love when married, would you

a divorce your partner and remarry?
b have a glorious affair but leave it at that?
c give up the new partner and suffer?

If you were lonely, would you

a marry the first person who looked interesting?
b learn to be self-sufficient but stay alert?
c wait till Mr. or Ms. Right came along?

If your marriage had problems, would you

a keep a lover on the side?
b suggest sex therapy?
c get a divorce?

If you disliked your body, would you

a learn to live with it?
b diet and exercise?
c have cosmetic surgery?

If your wooing went badly, would you

a regard it as a challenge?
b give up?
c get extremely depressed?

Your perfect partner has a flaw. Do you

a thank your lucky stars he's not worse?
b nag at her to change?
c feel that he's wrong for you?

A LOVER ARE YOU?

HOW DID YOU SCORE?

Mostly ⓐ *answers*
EASYGOING

You have such *joie de vivre* that you make the most out of whatever challenge comes your way. Don't get so carried away, however, that you lose sight of what's right for you.

See "The Easygoing Lover" on page 51.

Mostly ⓑ *answers*
BALANCED

A mature adult, you enjoy what you are given and you're not too ambitious about life or love. This makes you charming and easy to be with. Your only drawback is that you can be passive.

Go to "The Balanced Lover" on page 77.

Mostly ⓒ *answers*
PERFECTIONIST

Your sexual experiences often leave you feeling unsatisfied. Next time you feel a criticism coming on, switch over to a positive view. Having all kinds of experiences helps us to become better lovers.

Refer to "The Perfectionist Lover" on page 85.

WEEK
beginning.....................................

Monday

....

Tuesday

....

Wednesday

....

Thursday

....

Friday

Saturday

"Love is not the dying moan of a distant violin – it's the triumphant twang of a bedspring."

S.J. Perelman

Sunday

The ASSERTIVE *lover*

As an assertive lover, you tend to get what you want but without thinking of the cost. While it's good to have the confidence to achieve what you set out to obtain, it is also important to remember (especially where sex and loving are concerned) that human beings can be very sensitive souls. There's no point, for example, in trying to manipulate a partner into giving you oral sex if they will resent you afterward. If you are an assertive person, try to remember that other people may need gentle persuasion to come around to your way of thinking.

Rather than bullying, try a softer approach. This way your partner will come to appreciate your direct and decisive characteristics.

WEEK
beginning..................................

Monday

....

Tuesday

....

Wednesday

....

Thursday

....

Friday

Saturday

> "Men are those creatures with two legs and eight hands."
> *Jayne Mansfield*

Sunday

🖤 LOVE FACTS: *Different Strokes*

SEX DIFFERENCES
Men want sex with a lot of women. Women want a lot of sex with the man they love. This neat summary of male-female differences has been attributed to Lord Byron.

MAKING EYES
In tests where men had to rate two virtually identical photographs of a woman in order of attractiveness, it was the photo in which the woman's pupils were slightly enlarged that the subjects most often gave the highest rating.

LOVE RECOVERY
One study showed that 7 percent of men and 11 percent of women took a year or more to recover from the breakup of a long-term relationship.

HORMONES AND YOUR SEX DRIVE
Research suggests it's testosterone that provides men and women with both sexual drive and desire. Some doctors are hailing it as a new wonder cure for ailing libidos, but others are worried about side effects.

WEEK
beginning.................................

Monday

Tuesday

Wednesday

Thursday

Friday

Saturday

Sunday

ARIES *lovers*

♂ HE is difficult to get close to emotionally but has abundant sexual curiosity. He's always eager to experiment and a likely candidate for lovemaking in the office. He loves intercourse, and hates nothing more than when his partner doesn't climax. When choosing a mate, Aries man has a tendency to be influenced by looks more than personality, but is not put off by an inexperienced woman. In spite of his brash exterior, the Aries lover is more sensitive than he appears.

♀ SHE loves sexual variety, prefers quick and easy sex, but nevertheless adores the romance of hearing the words "I love you." Aries woman is also the female most likely to climax more than once in a session, but she's not averse to faking it. She loves the excitement of rough-and-tumble sex, and gets very turned on by making love in the great outdoors.

WEEK
beginning.............................

Monday

....

Tuesday

....

Wednesday

....

Thursday

....

Friday

Saturday

"Men ought to be more conscious of their bodies as an object of delight."
Germaine Greer

Sunday

The SUPPORTIVE *lover*

A lot of people adore a supportive lover like you because your genuine thoughtfulness and the actions you take on behalf of your lover make you a wonderful and valuable partner. But beware of being taken for granted, and be careful of stifling others by being too eager to help. Also, the supportive lover is very likely to be strong on skills such as empathy, and probably also has that rare talent, the ability to know when a lover needs to

be left alone, which is vital if you are to avoid being overly controlling. If you are a supportive lover, then your personality profile is one of the most mature. Your empathy and understanding translate into the bedroom to make a really sensitive and responsive lover who knows all the right moves to make without being told – a most valuable skill indeed!

WEEK
beginning.....................................

Monday

....

Tuesday

....

Wednesday

....

Thursday

....

Friday

Memorable Moments

Since most of us are sex addicts, we make love a lot. This means it can be difficult to look back and recall any particular incident – the mind blowing ones blend into the big picture. Don't lose touch with these special times. Put pen to paper and record them.

A FEW CLASSIC SCENARIOS:
Behind the filing cabinets
In a friend's apartment in the afternoon
In a cheap hotel in Paris

With an exciting stranger
When ending with a lover
That very special first time
On waking up, early in the morning

What are your memorable moments?

1 ....

2 ....

3 ....

Saturday

"Too much of a good thing can be wonderful."
Mae West

Sunday

WEEK
beginning...............................

Monday

Tuesday

Wednesday

Thursday

Friday

Saturday

"That was the most fun I ever had without laughing."
Woody Allen

Sunday

The ENTHUSIASTIC *lover*

Enthusiasm is a marvelous quality because it can overcome so many of the difficulties associated with depression and inertia. You breeze through your lovers' lives like a breath of fresh air, and sexually this makes you exciting and stimulating. As an enthusiast you would, of course, be well advised to ensure you actually know what you are doing, so it's worth studying. This is likely to be easy when sex is the subject. Your enjoyment of sexuality is likable and stimulating – you just need to make sure that your technical skills catch up with the rest of your performance.

After all, no amount of enthusiasm can make up for a lack of sensitivity, and there is more to being a skilled lover than simply being willing. Remember, less is often more in the world of the erotic, so add a touch of subtlety to improve your sexual technique.

WEEK
beginning.............................

Monday

Tuesday

Wednesday

Thursday

Friday

Sex in Unusual Situations

We have all heard of the Mile High Club; now you can create your own club. There are those who actually set out to have sex in the most bizarre surroundings, or just inches away from unsuspecting groups. Perhaps the danger of discovery is what gives an edge to sex like this.

HAVE YOU EVER HAD SEX:
- [ ] *on an airplane?*
- [ ] *in the ocean?*
- [ ] *at the gym?*
- [ ] *in the woods?*
- [ ] *in a crowded train?*
- [ ] *on a mountainside?*
- [ ] *in a nightclub?*
- [ ] *in a grassy meadow?*
- [ ] *under a waterfall?*
- [ ] *on a bus?*

List a few of your own exploits:

1 ....

2 ....

3 ....

4 ....

5 ....

Saturday

. . . .

Sunday

"Sex is dirty only when it's done right."
Woody Allen

WEEK
beginning...............................

Monday

....

Tuesday

....

Wednesday

....

Thursday

....

Friday

Saturday

Sunday

TAURUS *lovers*

♂ HE is a man of variety. He's turned on by most things, is noisy during lovemaking, and adores foreplay, yet on occasion may choose not to climax. Taurus men are likely to get along better with Taurus women than those from any other star sign. Once in love, Taurus man will stay dedicated and faithful. And despite the Taurean reputation for being tough, decisive leadership material, the Taurus lover is actually warm and cuddly.

♀ SHE is highly aroused by romantic events such as a candlelit meal or walking down a beach at sunset, likes her sex traditional (the good old missionary position), and feels that it should be a marriage of body and mind. Taurus woman has a fertile imagination, but can struggle to remain firmly rooted in reality.

WEEK
beginning.............................

Monday

....

Tuesday

....

Wednesday

....

Thursday

....

Friday

The EASYGOING *lover*

You are a relaxed, kind, and helpful person who is capable of accepting temperamental partners others find difficult.

This means that, if nothing else, your life is likely to be filled with surprises. Because you have a very laid-back personality, you are able to accept the highs and lows of sexual experience, reconciling a variety of contradictions and extremes. Consequently, sex may be either dull, tired, and uninspired, or extremely kinky. What's great is that you make all these extremes seem normal. As an easygoing lover you can also be very valuable in other areas. You will be relaxed when others are angry or impatient, and you are willing to talk through any problems instead of just flying off the handle. All of which makes you a great prize as a life-long partner.

Saturday

Sunday

HOW *jealous*

Your partner makes a new friend. Do you

a pursue a new friend yourself, in revenge?
b create scenes to get attention?
c do nothing because you have faith in yourself?

If your partner often stays out late, do you

a suspect the worst and spy on her?
b make it clear you dislike being left out?
c believe she is entitled to privacy?

Your partner dotes on the new baby. Do you

a feel left out and seek "friendship" elsewhere?
b put in a plea for some love too?
c think this is entirely natural?

Your partner thinks a film star is hot. Do you

a feel totally inadequate?
b feel amused?
c admire the actor yourself?

Your lover tries a new sex technique. Do you

a suspect he learned it with someone else?
b feel vaguely uneasy?
c agree happily and enjoy the inspiration?

Your partner has been in love before. Do you

a harp constantly about these former lovers?
b worry in case they are a threat?
c ask them over for dinner?

A LOVER ARE YOU?

HOW DID YOU SCORE?

Mostly ⓐ answers

DRAMATIC

You react dramatically when you think there is a threat to you and your love affair. You have a jealous temperament and you are easily hurt. An equally possessive partner will provide security.

See "The Dramatic Lover" on page 103.

Mostly ⓑ answers

LIBERAL

You don't want to feel jealous, and feel you bad when you do. Ask yourself – what are the insecurities that feed into this tendency? Don't worry, though; most people share your jealousy profile.

Turn to page 109 for "The Liberal Lover."

Mostly ⓒ answers

STRONG

You possess enough inner security to deal with your partner having a life of his own. You are able to tackle the occasional jealous twinge by inviting a "rival" to dinner instead of making a fuss.

See "The Strong Lover" on page 69.

WEEK
beginning...............................

Monday

> "It's not the men in my life that count, it's the life in my men."
> *Mae West*

Tuesday

Wednesday

Thursday

Friday

What Women Really Like

Women long for a skillful seduction, a sensitive pair of hands that gives the most sensational massage, a master of cunnilingus, a true romantic, a really good listener with a sympathetic ear, a lover who can be supportive and strong. Penis size is not as important as men think, but a good backside is a major turn-on. Status is an aphrodisiac, and powerful older men can be sexy by virtue of their masterful experience of the world. Conversely, youth and enthusiasm are often prized, too. A sense of humor is also a great turn-on.

What do *you* really like?

1 ....

2 ....

3 ....

4 ....

5 ....

6 ....

7 ....

8 ....

Saturday

Sunday

Did you feel the HEAT?

DANGER ZONE!

RED HOT!

HOT

HEATING UP

WARM

GETTING WARMER

COOL

This is the second of three orgasm charts to help you make a record of your sexual year. Use it to keep track of your orgasmic experiences. Write the date you had the orgasm in one of the colored bands on the Cool – Danger Zone! scale and add the sticker symbol that best defines the orgasm you had.

ORGASMIC SYMBOLS

Individual
Simultaneous
Prolonged
Multiple

LOVER'S NAME

WEEK
beginning.................................

Monday

....

Tuesday

....

Wednesday

....

Thursday

....

Friday

Saturday

. . . .

Sunday

GEMINI *lovers*

♂ HE is often picky about his sexual relationships, making his likes and dislikes very clear. He is charming, active, and gregarious, and rates shared interests as one of the most important features of a long-term love affair. He is initially attracted by a warm smile and a sexy laugh. He can be one of the hardest star signs to arouse, but once he's in the mood he's almost certainly the sexiest.

♀ SHE loves oral sex and gets very turned on by instant sex. Gemini woman is attracted to a wide range of sexual variations but unless she is truly convinced of her partner's honesty, she's unlikely to let her hair down. Once she does relax, though, she really enjoys her sex. She is the least likely of any of the star signs to fake an orgasm, and the most likely to be noisy when she reaches the heights of ecstasy.

WEEK
beginning...................................

Monday

....

Tuesday

....

Wednesday

....

Thursday

....

Friday

The DIRECT lover

There is no fooling around with the direct lover. You know exactly what you want and you go straight for it. Most partners like this because it means they know exactly where they stand. You offer quite a challenge because this straightforward approach means that your partner needs to be strong enough to cope. Softening up a little might be a good idea where sex is involved, or your partner may feel intimidated.

But, on the plus side, as a direct lover your honest nature should help you make your relationships stronger. Assuming, that is, that your partner is immune to your bluntness. In bed you may want to skip the foreplay and get straight down to business, and at the same time you are not afraid to tell your partner what you want. Once good communication is established in the bedroom, good sex is almost certain to follow.

Saturday

Sunday

"Women like brave men exceedingly, but audacious men still more."
Lemesles

WEEK
beginning......................................

Monday

. . . .

Tuesday

. . . .

Wednesday

. . . .

Thursday

. . . .

Friday

Saturday

Sunday

 My Best Loves

Undoubtedly the really good part of a romance is right at the start when you are madly in love and the object of your desires can do no wrong. This is the time when every joke is funny and even foolish little habits are so endearing. Here you can record those lovers who only had to look at you to make you wild with desire.

WHO WAS YOUR BEST LOVE, AND WHY? WAS IT:

☐ *The one who gave you great oral sex?*
☐ *The lover who lived on the edge?*
☐ *The one who was married?*
☐ *The lover who gave you the best sex?*
☐ *The one who was just passing through?*
☐ *The lover who was truly supportive?*
☐ *Someone else?*
(Be honest — who was it that really turned you on?)

List your best loves here:

....

....

....

....

....

WEEK
beginning.................................

Monday

....

Tuesday

....

Wednesday

....

Thursday

....

Friday

Saturday

· ·

Sunday

CANCER *lovers*

♂ HE adores lovemaking and because he's likely to turn sex into a favorite hobby, he's also a very good lover. Cancer man is attracted to all sorts of women regardless of their looks. But it's quality rather than quantity that counts the most, since his sex drive is quite low. In one respect, Cancer man is the envy of the zodiac: he's the most likely to experience multiple orgasms. This is a rare treat for men, so he's lucky.

♀ SHE wants to be committed and has little time for quick flings. Although she's not desperate for a lot of sex, she longs to experiment with one partner. She is more likely than average to be sexually attracted to other women since she is so open-minded. As a water sign, she enjoys aquatic locations for sex, especially the tub or shower. And she just loves to be soaped from head to toe by her man.

WEEK
beginning...............................

Monday

....

Tuesday

....

Wednesday

....

Thursday

....

Friday

My Worst Loves

Finding the right lover can be a path strewn with obstacles of every sort. We negotiate a constant tightrope to discover Mr. or Ms. Right, and along the way there are bound to be some real catastrophes. Summon up your courage and make a record of those embarrassing liaisons. At least you can look back and laugh, can't you?

WHO WAS YOUR NIGHTMARE LOVER?

☐ *The one who always wore socks in bed?*
☐ *The one who left the toilet door open?*
☐ *The lover who had too many old flames?*
☐ *The lover who had poor hygiene?*
☐ *The one who didn't believe in foreplay?*
☐ *The one who was still married?*
☐ *The one who ate too much garlic?*
☐ *The one who bored you to tears?*
☐ *The lover who was a football fanatic?*
☐ *The one who robbed you blind?*

OR WERE THEY EVEN WORSE?
(Get it out of your system, and have a good laugh with your current lover)

1 ....

2 ....

3 ....

4 ....

Saturday

Sunday

"No sex is better than bad sex."
Germaine Greer

WEEK
beginning....................................

Monday

. . . .

Tuesday

. . . .

Wednesday

. . . .

Thursday

. . . .

Friday

Saturday

> "Macho does not prove mucho."
> *Zsa Zsa Gabor*

Sunday

The STRONG *lover*

Nothing can rattle the strong lover. You have developed a kind of inner courage that allows you to deal with your difficulties without getting upset and lets you provide a shoulder to cry on when things get tough. Best of all, you are unlikely to get jealous about either petty things or real infidelities. This doesn't mean that your partner can get away with lying and cheating. Instead, you might simply pack your bags one day and walk out the door. If this happens your lover could discover that he has lost a solid and reliable partner, someone well worth holding on to. But then, the strong and silent type isn't necessarily everyone's cup of tea. In bed you are not overtly wild and explicit, but your lover can sense deep currents of passion that flow beneath the surface. The understated can be very erotic in its own right – this is your appeal.

WEEK
beginning..............................

Monday

> "Erotica happens in the head."
> *Margaret Reynolds*

Tuesday

Wednesday

Thursday

Friday

My Favorite Erotic Books

Both men and women are turned on by erotic literature. Women tend to be aroused by the more romantic "bodice-ripper" novels, while men go for tougher stuff. But either way, swapping titles can be a "novel" route to great shared sex.

CLASSICS OF EROTICA
The erotica hall of fame is littered with greats, many of which caused a scandal in their day. They run the gamut from Lady Chatterley's Lover *right up to modern-day classics by writers such as Nancy Friday. Why not try reading some? You might be surprised at how exciting they are.*

Make a list of your favorite works of erotic literature and compare them with your lover's top seven:

1 ....

2 ....

3 ....

4 ....

5 ....

6 ....

7 ....

Saturday

· ·

Sunday

HOW *caring* a

When it's your lover's birthday, do you

a remember to celebrate?
b forget but cover up at the last minute?
c forget entirely?

If your partner looks tired, do you

a let him sleep because he needs the rest?
b seduce him into feeling sexy after all?
c insist on sex as your right?

If your partner is upset, do you

a encourage her to sob on your shoulder?
b offer to punch the person who's upset her?
c threaten to leave if she doesn't shut up?

If you and your partner both work, do you

a share the shopping and cooking equally?
b rely on him to do everything at home?
c treat the house like a garbage dump?

If asked to do something you dislike, do you

a agree because your partner loves it?
b do it really grudgingly?
c refuse outright?

If a partner is too sexually "way out," do you

a suggest you both go for counseling?
b feel you have to put up with it?
c drop her like a hot potato?

LOVER ARE YOU?

HOW DID YOU SCORE?

Mostly ⓐ answers
CARING

You are one of those rare people who takes time to think about your partner's feelings. You see a lover in terms of pure romance even when he behaves badly. Just don't get taken for granted.

See page 93 for more on "The Caring Lover."

Mostly ⓑ answers
ENDURING

You are able to work through difficulties, and this is comforting to your partner. But you find it hard to anticipate your partner's feelings. Try to plan your love life so that it doesn't take you by surprise.

See "The Enduring Lover" on page 113.

Mostly ⓒ answers
ASSERTIVE

Although you don't mean to be thoughtless, you can end up hurting your partner. Your route to change would be to curb your assertive behavior, and to try and see her point of view.

Go to "The Assertive Lover" on page 35.

WEEK
beginning.................................

Monday

....

Tuesday

....

Wednesday

....

Thursday

....

Friday

Saturday

"Sex without love is a meaningless experience, but as meaningless experiences go, it's one of the best."
Woody Allen

Sunday

 Memorable Quickies

There's no law that says sex has to be serious, romantic, and drawn-out. Spontaneous sex is very often the reverse. Hour-long sessions are all very well, but a "knee-trembler" can be just as much fun, and takes only a fraction of the time! There's room in everyone's relationship for a little of this, so don't be a prude – get down to it!

HAVE YOU DONE IT:
- [ ] *In a car?*
- [ ] *Across the kitchen table?*
- [ ] *In your parents' house?*
- [ ] *On the beach?*
- [ ] *In a photo booth?*
- [ ] *Up against a tree?*
- [ ] *At a major tourist attraction?*
- [ ] *In the shower?*
- [ ] *In the office?*
- [ ] *On the dance floor?*

List a few of your own:

1 ....

2 ....

3 ....

4 ....

5 ....

WEEK
beginning.....................................

Monday

....

Tuesday

....

Wednesday

....

Thursday

....

Friday

The BALANCED *lover*

As a balanced lover, you have a very high degree of basic common sense. Skill in understanding just how stable or volatile a sexual relationship can be is of premium value when it comes to the tricky negotiation of a long-lasting love. Remember, using your head is at least as important as using your heart. The downside of having such equilibrium is that the well-balanced lover sometimes feels he or she is missing out because his or her emotional life seems predictable. But it's a mistake to regret this. You shouldn't confuse steadiness with tedium, or stability with dullness. Imagine life with a drama king or queen, and then stop and reassess your anxieties. Most men and women would give their eye-teeth for a stable, balanced partner with your kind of common sense and level-headed approach to life.

Saturday

Sunday

"Men and women, women and men. It will never work."
Erica Jong

WEEK
beginning.............................

Monday

....

Tuesday

....

Wednesday

....

Thursday

....

Friday

Saturday

"The true feeling of sex is that of a deep intimacy, but above all of a deep complicity."
James Dickey

Sunday

LOVE FACTS: *Deepening Love*

WHAT IS ROMANCE FOR?

One suggestion is that romance acts as the supporting girders of a new love affair, and once the relationship is established, it holds it together. An occasional sensitive word, a bunch of flowers, or a thoughtful supper for two . . . corny as these things may sound, they help to build the romantic edifice.

KEEPING IT UP

Researchers have shown that when a man believes a woman is turned on by the effect he has on her, his own sexual excitement increases greatly. This may happen even if his belief is incorrect and he's fooling himself.

THE MATURE LOVER

As people mature they become more realistic about love. They may want to recreate the feelings of that first love affair, but now they are far more aware of the inadequacies of infatuation. They know that it can be short-lived and superficial. It is not that the passion or romance of their relationship dies, it is simply tempered by a deeper, stronger love based on enduring foundations.

WEEK
beginning...............................

Monday

....

Tuesday

....

Wednesday

....

Thursday

....

Friday

Saturday

....

Sunday

LEO *lovers*

♂ HE goes in for sexuality as if it were an Olympic event. He values sex profoundly, viewing it as the ultimate reward. But in spite of his high batting average, he's rarely completely satisfied, usually wanting more. His high sex drive suggests a tendency to be anxious, since this is often the product of tension. But his partners can help him to relax by indulging his desire for extended foreplay. Though he may take time to get started, once he does there's no stopping him.

♀ SHE is also highly sexed, but not as driven. Nevertheless, Leo woman worries that she may not always be meeting her lover's high standards and looks for ways to make herself sexier. Learning to relax a little would be worthwhile, so that she can let her fantasy life out into the open and start making it come true.

Did you feel the HEAT?

DANGER ZONE!

RED HOT!

HOT

HEATING UP

WARM

GETTING WARMER

COOL

This is the third of three orgasm charts to help you make a record of your sexual year. Use it to keep track of your orgasmic experiences. Write the date you had the orgasm in one of the colored bands on the Cool – Danger Zone! scale and add the sticker symbol that best defines the orgasm you had.

ORGASMIC SYMBOLS

⚡ *Individual*
💕 *Simultaneous*
⭐ *Prolonged*
💥 *Multiple*

LOVER'S NAME

WEEK
beginning...............................

Monday

....

Tuesday

....

Wednesday

....

Thursday

....

Friday

Saturday

"Men make love more intensely at twenty, but make love better, however, at thirty."
Catherine II of Russia

Sunday

The PERFECTIONIST *lover*

Being a perfectionist, you want your partner to be perfect so badly that you overlook the value of your real-life lover. It may be that you are simply a little too much of an idealist when it comes to your relationships, or that you possess romantic fantasies that give you expectations that are unrealistic. This is a pity because it means your relationship will never feel completely right and a marvelous lover might well be lost. Lightening up and letting go are the messages most perfectionists need to take to heart if they are to mature as lovers and avoid the pitfalls outlined above. Where the issue is sex, this means accepting your partner's technique in the bedroom and seeing all its positive sides instead of focusing only on negative aspects. At least your own drive for perfection means that you will always do your best to provide perfect sex!

WEEK
beginning.................................

Monday

Tuesday

Wednesday

Thursday

Friday

Dressing for Sex

Both men and women can be bashful about their choice of erotic clothing: men because they fear being seen as too effeminate; women because they fear being thought too experienced. But both sexes can enjoy the subtle feel of silks and satins against bare skin. The rule to apply is to believe that what goes on in private, in bed, between consenting couples, is OK. After all, a sexy get-up can be a singular turn-on.

WOULD YOU LIKE HER TO WEAR:
☐ *A garter belt and stockings?*
☐ *A black bustier?*
☐ *A silk teddy?*
☐ *A fur coat with nothing underneath?*
☐ *A schoolgirl's uniform?*
☐ *Fishnet stockings?*
☐ *Virginal white?*
☐ *A thong?*
☐ *Nothing at all?*

WOULD YOU LIKE HIM TO WEAR:
☐ *Cartoon-style boxers?*
☐ *Black slip-style briefs?*
☐ *Red silk boxers?*
☐ *A black silk robe?*
☐ *Leather gear?*
☐ *Rubber bondage gear?*
☐ *Black silk pajamas?*
☐ *A posing pouch?*
☐ *Nothing at all?*

Saturday

"My husband is German. Every night I get dressed up as Poland and he invades me."
Bette Midler

Sunday

WEEK
beginning.................................

Monday

....

Tuesday

....

Wednesday

....

Thursday

....

Friday

Saturday

Sunday

VIRGO *lovers*

♂ HE is a perfectionist, always wanting sex to be ideal. For him, less is more, and he believes that abstinence promotes greater sexual sensitivity. Ideally, Virgo man would prefer that sex just fit into place among all the many other aspects of life. But the right woman can tempt him, especially if she has a businesslike attitude that matches his own. The right approach is more important to Virgo man than good looks or a shapely body.

♀ SHE is a bashful person in general who can also be a shy lover. She will spend a lot of time daydreaming and often longs for a muscular male who will sweep her off her feet and take care of her erotic needs. She will only bestow her love on a man who has gone to a lot of trouble to prove that he's worth it. In many ways modern romance has passed her by – she needs to be wooed in an old-fashioned way, with gifts and flowers, and plenty of attention.

WEEK
beginning...................................

Monday

Tuesday

Wednesday

Thursday

Friday

My Favorite Aphrodisiacs

Most of the traditional aphrodisiacs either don't work or are bad for your health; for example, Spanish fly can be lethal. And nowadays substances that genuinely *are* mood-altering are usually prohibited. However, we all invariably have our own particular food, drink, smell, or flavor that we associate with instant arousal and fantastic sex.

WHAT WORKS FOR YOU? IS IT ONE OF THESE:

- ☐ *Oysters?*
- ☐ *Strawberries?*
- ☐ *Chocolate?*
- ☐ *Certain flowers?*
- ☐ *Exotic incense?*
- ☐ *Caviar?*
- ☐ *An expensive perfume?*
- ☐ *The scent of massage oil?*
- ☐ *Rich ice cream?*

Make your own list of favorite scents and flavors, and share it with your lover. It may provide food for thought!

1 ....

2 ....

3 ....

4 ....

Saturday

"Great food is like great sex – the more you have, the more you want."
Gael Green

Sunday

WEEK
beginning............................

Monday

....

Tuesday

....

Wednesday

....

Thursday

....

Friday

Saturday

Sunday

The CARING lover

Men and women who genuinely care about others' welfare and feelings are lamentably rare creatures. The best way in which to show such caring is to act quietly on your beliefs, thereby making yourself indispensable in the most erotic and thoughtful way. You don't waste time telling the world your feelings; instead you get on with your life. Yet because you don't look for attention you suffer the possibility of being taken for granted. This is one of the most damaging things that can happen in a relationship. So remember to ask for your own needs to be met as well. A little selfishness could be better for both of you in the long run. The chances are that your partner will be pleased to discover what you really like, and how best to turn you on. You may find that the quality of your sex life shows radical improvement.

WEEK
beginning..............................

Monday

....

Tuesday

....

Wednesday

....

Thursday

....

Friday

Saturday

Sunday

What Men Really Like

Men fantasize about long legs in high heels, curvaceous bodies, generous breasts, women who know how to use their fingertips with skill, who are not afraid of being direct, who take the initiative, and want to be the woman on top. Most men wouldn't say no to lovemaking with an oral sex genius or a partner who is ready and willing to experiment. But, above all, a man wants his woman to lend an understanding ear to his foibles, fetishes, and fantasies, to massage his ego, and to make him feel like a king.

What do *you* really like?

1 ....

2 ....

3 ....

4 ....

5 ....

6 ....

7 ....

8 ....

WEEK
beginning..............................

Monday

....

Tuesday

"I like men to behave like men – strong and childish."
Françoise Sagan

....

Wednesday

....

Thursday

....

Friday

The INDEPENDENT *lover*

You are so accustomed to caring for yourself that you forget there's anyone else in the world. The difficulty with this is that your partner is likely to feel extremely left out. And relationships don't last long when they are lived on that basis. If you are self-sufficient, you need to formulate an effective program of thinking about your lover and considering his or her demands, before planning the best solution. This way you can look after your own needs without the feeling that you are making too many concessions to your partner's desires.

Being more considerate will satisfy you more in the long term. A positive aspect of your character is that as an independent lover you know your own mind, your likes, and dislikes. This is the first step toward being a better lover.

Saturday

• •

Sunday

WEEK
beginning.................................

Monday

....

Tuesday

....

Wednesday

....

Thursday

....

Friday

Saturday

· ·

Sunday

LIBRA *lovers*

♂ HE wants a lot of sex with a lot of partners, and generally enjoys making love more than four times a week, giving him one of the highest libidos in the zodiac. Yet he may find it hard to meet a woman who suits him emotionally, perhaps because he sees sex as the yardstick of a relationship. But Libra man's defining feature is his love of luxury. This includes romantic meals, sensual massages, exotic locations and plush settings for his sumptuous fantasies.

♀ SHE is the reverse of the Libra male, being highly unlikely to go for multiple partners. Instead she prefers a strictly faithful, old-fashioned marriage. But within wedlock she can be sexually free-spirited and adventurous, provided her partner can keep her interested and stimulated.

HOW *intimate*

If your partner is anxious, do you

a tell yourself this has nothing to do with you?
b solve the problem yourself?
c help her improve things for herself?

Do you sense with your partner that

a you are complete opposites?
b you have little in common?
c you are a good match?

When you date, do you

a feel bored when it's your turn to listen?
b show off about your own amazing qualities?
c enjoy talking about interests in common?

In a crisis, do you

a say "I told you so"?
b not really know how to help?
c bend over backwards to be supportive?

In bed, do you

a have little idea what your partner really wants?
b make informed guesses about what will please?
c feel as though his mind and body are yours?

After sex, do you feel

a like getting up and going?
b like falling asleep immediately?
c at peace holding your partner?

A LOVER ARE YOU?

HOW DID YOU SCORE?

Mostly ⓐ answers
INDEPENDENT

You are a bit of a loner, and you can get so wrapped up in yourself that your partner feels you are not there. Don't lose your partner by confusing sexual intercourse with lovemaking.

See "The Independent Lover" on page 97.

Mostly ⓑ answers
PLEASING

You want to be a good mate, but you sometimes go too far, and your well-intended actions may seem smothering or controlling. Your overwhelming desire to please may hide insecurities.

Turn to "The Pleasing Lover" on page 19.

Mostly ⓒ answers
SUPPORTIVE

Your ability to be supportive and friendly inspires warmth and loyalty in return. And you are mature enough to see that even if you love someone you shouldn't step in and do everything.

See "The Supportive Lover" on page 41.

WEEK
beginning.....................................

Monday

Tuesday

Wednesday

Thursday

Friday

The DRAMATIC lover

The dramatic lover lives like there's no tomorrow. In practical terms, this means that you may overreact in an emotional way to what are often completely normal situations. However, it also means that life is ceaselessly fascinating as seen through your eyes. The negative aspect is that the partner who finds him or herself coping with this variety of emotions can get worn out. We don't all live life as a soap opera, and few of us have enough energy to keep up with those who do. In other words, you must try and calm down and sort out the trivial from the earth-shattering. It may be a cliché, but do your best not to make a mountain out of a mole-hill. The positive side of your character is that your flair for the dramatic can transform the bedroom into an erotic theater, where you and your lover can act out all the wildest fantasies you can come up with!

Saturday

Sunday

"Ducking for apples – change one letter and it's the story of my life."
Dorothy Parker

WEEK
beginning.................................

Monday

Tuesday

Wednesday

Thursday

Friday

Saturday

"Is that a gun in your pocket or are you just glad to see me?"
Mae West

Sunday

My Most Awkward Moments

Even the most decorous lover will eventually slip up. You may be passionate about your new partner but romantically whisper the name of your ex in his or her ear. You may have arranged the perfect romantic dinner but find that food poisoning sends you rushing for the bathroom. The truth about sex is that it can often be undignified. At least laughter is the best aphrodisiac.

HAVE ANY OF THESE EVER HAPPENED TO YOU?

☐ *The dog interrupting you during sex*
☐ *Breaking wind at the peak of passion*
☐ *Forgetting about the cleaning lady*
☐ *Falling out of bed as you climax*
☐ *The alarm going off just as you do*
☐ *Your mother visits unexpectedly*
☐ *Bursting into laughter during oral sex*
☐ *Being caught wearing your ratty undies*

What classic mishaps have you and your lover racked up?

1 ....

2 ....

3 ....

4 ....

WEEK
beginning.................................

Monday

....

Tuesday

....

Wednesday

....

Thursday

....

Friday

Saturday

. . . .

Sunday

SCORPIO *lovers*

♂ HE is widely believed to be the sexiest male in the zodiac and tries hard to live up to this reputation. He is passionate and temperamental, though unfortunately his volatile character means that women find it hard to commit to him. Also, he can be picky about sex, with a taste for the unusual that leads him to get bored by traditional positions and practices. Scorpio man believes that variety is the spice of life, and he wants all the spice he can get!

♀ SHE feels strongly that sexuality is central to her entire life, believing that her every mood is affected by how often she climaxes. Her interest in men is more physical than emotional, and she is likely to have many lovers in her lifetime. She can take something special from each of them and incorporate into her own sexual vocabulary, which makes her probably the most inventive and varied female lover in the whole zodiac.

WEEK
beginning.....................................

Monday

....

Tuesday

....

Wednesday

....

Thursday

....

Friday

Saturday

> "I'll wager you that in ten years it will be fashionable again to be a virgin."
>
> *Barbara Cartland*

Sunday

The LIBERAL *lover*

You are someone who believes that partners should be tolerant of each other's behavior. In other words, lovers ought to be able to accept anything that their partner dishes out. The trouble with this attitude is that sometimes a partner's bad behavior may provoke a violent gut reaction, which can be difficult to mesh with your own beliefs. You would be wise to realize that there's nothing wrong in having strong feelings about the person you love. Most people are jealous some of the time. In feeling like this, you are simply being the same as most of the human race! If you are as broad-minded in bed as in life, your partner will find you willing to experiment, and open-minded to any move that might improve your sex life. Come to terms with your stronger feelings and embrace your more erotic side.

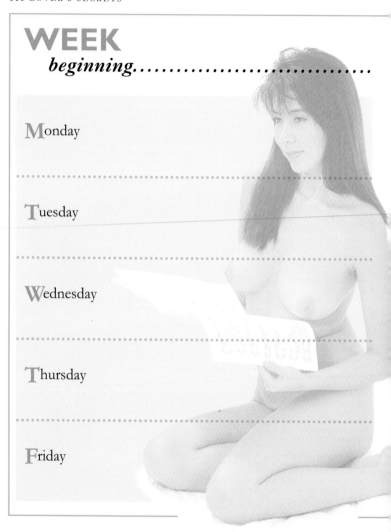

WEEK
beginning.................................

Monday

Tuesday

Wednesday

Thursday

Friday

Music to Make Love by

Remember how everyone bought recordings of Ravel's "Bolero" in 1979? Why does music have such an effect on us? Is it the associations we make whenever we hear our song? Next time you hear a tune that gets your blood racing, make a note of it on this page and try it out in the bedroom.

Artist: Track:

1 ....

2 ....

3 ....

4 ....

5 ....

Saturday

....

Sunday

"If music be the food of love, play on."
Shakespeare

WEEK
beginning.................................

Monday

....

Tuesday

....

Wednesday

....

Thursday

....

Friday

The ENDURING *lover*

The ability to doggedly hang on in a relationship when it gets tough is very valuable, and as an enduring lover you can do just this. You have the commitment and the force of will to last out the bad times and to help your relationship through any troubled periods. But besides being tenacious, you need to develop skills that can improve a situation. This may apply to what actually happens in your sex life. Being capable of providing inexhaustible sensual massage, or of sustaining prolonged sex for hours at a time, gets boring if not much else happens. Quality is more important than quantity in the sexual world. You need to try and build on your emotional staying power to become an expert in the ways of eroticism.

Saturday

Sunday

"Never miss a chance to have sex or appear on television."
Gore Vidal

HOW *playful*

Do you like

a having fun at parties?
b candlelit dinners?
c formal occasions?

Before going to bed for the first time, do you

a make your lover helpless with laughter?
b lead your lover by the hand?
c discreetly brush your teeth?

Does your sexual approach include

a wrestling?
b gazing into your lover's eyes?
c massaging your lover's body?

If your lover is not in the mood, do you

a tease him into a different frame of mind?
b accept it and snuggle up instead?
c take it personally?

If you have a lover's quarrel, do you

a make up easily?
b sulk for days?
c see this as part of a bigger problem?

Does your sexual pattern consist of

a variety depending upon mood and energy?
b emotional and mental buildup before sex?
c mainly straight sexual intercourse?

A LOVER ARE YOU?

HOW DID YOU SCORE?

Mostly ⓐ answers
DYNAMIC

You are enormous fun to be with, endearing to everyone, and easy to trust. Also, you can help more timid partners through what might otherwise turn out to be embarassing moments.

See "The Dynamic Lover" on page 9.

Mostly ⓑ answers
ROMANTIC

You are such a romantic that opportunities for fun in lovemaking sometimes pass you by. Learn to fool around more, including lightening up and becoming more playful in bed.

Turn to "The Romantic Lover" on page 117.

Mostly ⓒ answers
SENSITIVE

You feel secure through correctness. You can appreciate a good joke but probably only in the right setting. You could probably gain a lot from loosening up a little.

Go to "The Sensitive Lover" on page 15.

WEEK
beginning.....................................

Monday

....

Tuesday

....

Wednesday

....

Thursday

....

Friday

The ROMANTIC *lover*

Rose-tinted glasses and a vivid imagination are the attributes of the romantic lover. Life with a romantic man may appear to be every woman's dream since it probably really does include being swept off your feet and carried to the nuptial bed, while a romantic woman will make her lover feel like a king. If you are lucky enough to be wooed by a romantic, expect bouquets, chocolates, and loads of other thoughtful presents.

The downside to a romantic lover is that romance isn't always practical; so if you are an incorrigible romantic, do try not to throw your partner on to a bed if it's likely to collapse, and, should you send them flowers, make sure they are not allergic to the blooms! Above all, you will both need to work hard to ensure the romance in your relationship does not fade away with time.

Saturday

· ·

Sunday

WEEK
beginning.................................

Monday

....

Tuesday

....

Wednesday

....

Thursday

....

Friday

Saturday

Sunday

SAGITTARIUS *lovers*

♂ HE is self-critical and often more motivated by success than sex. Sagittarius man is turned on by power in the workplace and financial rewards. His business sense means that he expects his women to give him value for money. He also likes sex with as few complications as possible, preferring to limit his emotional investment in a relationship and just enjoy the sex.

♀ SHE is not as confident as she appears and her hang-ups may crop up at rather inconvenient moments. She likes her sex life to be comfortable – not for her eroticism in the great outdoors. Although unlikely to be sexually adventurous, she enjoys being the one who initiates sex, and tends to favor woman-on-top positions that enable her to control the tempo of sex.

WEEK
beginning................................

Monday

....

Tuesday

....

Wednesday

....

Thursday

....

Friday

Do your PROFILES *match?*

One of the predictors for successful partnership is that you should have a lot in common. The best way of comparing behavior and mood is for both you and your partner to complete the quizzes that are included in this diary and to compare your answers. The more of them that match, the more likely you are to sustain a gorgeous, romantic, long-lasting love affair. Never fear, though, if they don't match. You can use the differences to help you adapt to one another's likes and dislikes and to radically improve your sex and love lives. You may have discovered, for example, that while you like to take your time over going to bed, your partner prefers to tear his or her clothes off on entering the bedroom, or that while you like to be noisy, your lover is shy. You need to match up your love modes somewhere in the middle.

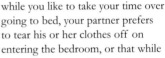

Saturday

· ·

Sunday

WEEK
beginning...............................

Monday

....

Tuesday

....

Wednesday

....

Thursday

....

Friday

"A man is often too young to marry, but never too old to fall in love."
Finnish proverb

LOVE FACTS: *Starting Again*

GETTING OVER IT

If you have an extrovert character, a new relationship and even simple physical distance could heal the damage of a lost love. Introverts recover more slowly, as they are far more likely to suffer from pining and persevering in their attempts to cling to their relationship.

THE OLDER LOVER

Middle-aged men and women can experience new love as being so profound and erotic that it's even better than the first relationship.

MARRYING FOR MONEY

If, next time around, you hanker for someone wealthy, make sure you mix in millionaire's circles. Studies show that we tend to fall for people with whom we spend the most time.

THE EROTICS OF LOVE

One of the best ways to pep up a flagging sex life and start afresh in the bedroom is to inject a bit of fantasy, perhaps by introducing role playing games or using some sexy and erotic costumes.

Saturday

· ·

Sunday

WEEK
beginning.................................

Monday

....

Tuesday

....

Wednesday

....

Thursday

....

Friday

Saturday

"Graze on my lips; and if those hills be dry, stray lower, where the pleasant fountains lie."
Shakespeare

Sunday

The PERFECT lover

Now that you've completed the six quizzes and compared notes with your lover, you should have some idea about what sort of a lover you are – what sexual profile you have. Does yours match with your self-image? How is it different, and how would you like to change it if you could? Finding the answers to questions like these could help you take your first steps toward becoming a perfect lover. You can learn to acquire the special blend of characteristics and qualities that are ideal for meeting the needs of both you and your partner. The essential thing is to strike a balance between the two. If you can identify these qualities and work toward them, you will feel more confident and happier in yourself, and this self-assurance will in turn enable you to become a more skilled, sensitive lover.

WEEK
beginning.....................................

Monday

Tuesday

Wednesday

Thursday

Friday

Saturday

> "Sex is a beautiful thing between two people. Between *five*, it's fantastic."
> *Woody Allen*

Sunday

 How Was Your Year?

Looking back, the year tends to fall into good or bad categories, and the best measure of what makes a good year is probably personal happiness. Try listing all the positive events in your amorous year to assess whether it is a time to remember.

WHAT WERE THE OUTSTANDING MOMENTS OF YOUR YEAR?

Romantic

Sexual

Intimate

INDEX